A SMALL BOOK ABOUT
LARGE GROUP GAMES

Karl Rohnke

KENDALL/HUNT PUBLISHING COMPANY
4050 Westmark Drive   Dubuque, Iowa 52002

All illustrations, once again, by Toshiyuki Morozumi of Kanagawa, Japan.

Thanks to Deb and Gus Pausz for taking the time to read the text and for their insightful comments.

More than thanks (ongoing gratitude perhaps) to my wife Gloree for her unflagging commitment to quality and her creative text on processing large groups.

Author photo by Nicki Hall

ISBN 0-7872-9704-6

Library of Congress Control Number: 2002112226

Printed in the United States of America
10 9 8 7 6 5 4 3 2 1

Contents

Peruse These Paragraphs Before You Buy This Book

If you bought this book sight unseen, (or did not read this page until you got home) and the content is not what you expected or need, mail or UPS the book to me at the address below and I will personally reimburse you for the cost of the book and shipping.

The reason for the italicized sentence above isn't because I'm concerned about the quality or content of *Small Book...*, it's because *ALL* of the games and initiatives included can be found in other books I've authored.*

In *Small Book...*I've collected those games and initiatives that I find work best with large groups. For each activity write up I have included set up, rules, and facilitating tips. Perhaps more significantly, every activity in this book is on my short list of BEST games or initiative problems.

Programmatically applied games or initiatives, for large or small groups, function as a vehicle to achieve your educational goals, and honestly, the vehicle you choose doesn't matter as much as the way you approach the situation, venue, and most importantly the people.

* All writing in this book is original and current.

Karl Rohnke
Townshend, VT
August 2002

Preface

For years I had been trying to convince interested teachers and trainers that adventure games and initiative problems were best presented to "smaller" groups of 15-20 participants. Part of that conviction had to do with a then unrecognized facilitator survival mind set, I selfishly didn't want to put up with the imagined hassles of dealing with a large group; at that point, I wasn't even sure what "large" meant. So I smoothly and convincingly talked about the benefits of participant involvement in a smaller group, emphasizing the opportunity for individual attention, and the rapport developed twixt teacher and learner, etc.

In 1991, Project Adventure, a company I had been associated with for the preceding 20 years, was celebrating their 20th anniversary. As part of that double-decade milestone, a one day celebration had been planned for anyone who had been previously associated with the Project, just a good old get together for sharing, laughter, reminiscing and *cementing future business contacts!*

Carefully chosen adventure oriented time slots had been meticulously planned for the day (slide show, technical presentations, hands-on academic schemes) with veteran practitioners being highlighted. I was asked to present a series of classic games and initiatives, golden oldies that had struck a playful cord during the early years. I said, "Sure." and left it at that, after all, games are games. It wasn't until we heard there might be upwards of one-hundred (100!) people attending that I began an in-brain, (never let 'em see you sweat) angst ridden argument with myself as to why that many people would ruin the activity and the presentation. I was easy to convince.

As it turned out there were closer to two-hundred people, and, of course, the large group activities presented that day were all well received. If people are coming to have a good time the word *large,* as it's applied to numbers of people, is relatively unimportant. These "casts of thousands" perceive a facilitator as their conduit to fun and will support that person to an extraordinary extent IF you don't get in the way of their FUNN. To wit:

- Define the rules exactly and clearly, but keep the presentation short and simple. Game players did not come to hear you talk.

- Let the game or activity happen. If you chose a good game, a fun oriented group will take care of themselves with minimum guidance from you.

- Totally involve yourself in the activity. Don't take over, but let the group see that you are not only willing to play, but that you really like what's going on.

- If you have a cool new *Fox 40* whistle, leave it home. Whistles remind players of rule heavy, win/lose scenarios.

*FUNN — An acronym (Functional Understanding's Not Necessary) crafted to deflate some of the seriousness applied to fun.

As time went by, conference session groups became larger and larger. Conveners no longer inquired, "Can you handle thirty?" It was more like, "Is forty OK?" Today, 50-75 participants isn't unusual and for the short term, (60-90 minutes) even groups numbering in the hundreds can have an excellent experience if you have the confidence and technology (chutzpah and sound system) to let that happen.

Which brings us to the word *edutainment*. I can't remember where I first heard the word, but someone said I was good at it. There's no dictionary definition of this literary amalgam, but you get a passing idea of intent by combining, *education* and *entertainment*.

Is *edutainment* a valid means of educating, in other words, can entertainment be part of educating? No question in my mind, as people willingly come back to hear more of what you have to offer *if* their first encounter with you had some fun (read, enjoyment) attached. That doesn't mean you have to develop a shtick or think of your class as a gig, but it does indicate that effective educating involves more than text and lecture.

Leo Buscaglia said, "Hug someone, be outrageous..." Basically, I'm not a huggy person, but I've been known to be occasionally outrageous. Outrageous in this context does not mean obnoxious. You do not have to consistently draw wide-eyed attention to yourself, but histrionically presenting *The Dog Shake* at the right time (sequencing correctly) can have a lasting affect on how students perceive you as *their* educator, but more importantly sets a programmatic anticipation of, what's coming next. Encourage that anticipation of "What's next?" rather than engendering the dreaded, "Oh no, not that again!"

Manipulations of a Three Decade Edutainer

I've done and said things over the years as an adventure facilitator that I now realize were the result of experience, instinct, and on-the-job training. Here's a fairly comprehensive collection of some facilitator/game-leader tips and tricks that may or may not be familiar.

✳ Getting Started

- Casually (conversationally) make a comment to the collecting group about something weird you saw, experienced, or heard about. (Did you know that a giraffe *does* have vocal cords?) Get their interest without trying to get their interest. (*Sesquipedalian* refers to the use of large words.) You don't have to wear a clown's red nose to stand out or be amusing. Develop rapport before you develop program.

- As attention is gradually drawn to you, THE facilitator, try not to be ordinary. Do something mildly outrageous. Show them a fleece ball, say a few supportive words about its safe use, then creatively propel that soft sphere to someone in the group (behind the back lob, bounce it off your biceps, etc.) Ask that person to creatively return it. Or, casually place a *Woosh* ring on your head while making introductory comments. Ask everyone in the group to demonstrate a short lip whistle. Demonstrate the first whistle, making sure not to sound too good. After they have made their effort (amidst much predictable laughter) say "Nice going." And move on to something else. Don't debrief the whistle! This is a *why* break, not a *how* moment.

- Set up an intimate atmosphere by suggesting that everyone come closer, because, if given half a chance people in a large group will drift toward the back of a presentation area. When they start getting close I might say "That's close enough!" in a faux threatening tone. It's worth a smile and the occasional laugh, but more importantly it breaks the predictable presenter mold. Also, no-contact clustering will save your voice and cause everyone to comfortably compress his/her personal space.

- During the first few minutes of "getting to know me," talk directly to individuals. Make eye contact with lots of people who are looking at you. You are not talking to a group, you are communicating with a group of potential friends who happen to be standing or sitting near you.

- Use self deprecating humor—senior moments (in my case), fumbling on an initiative presentation, forgetting names, losing track of what you just said during a talk... Don't appear stupid, rather occasionally addled, i.e. human, just like them.

- Use the first few contact minutes to utilize your nervousness (if you aren't nervous something's wrong). Say something that's topically interesting, something from the daily news. There's always a bizarre happenstance or scenario on the second or third page. You have nothing to forget or be nervous about if initial verbal sharing consists of interesting conversational banter. If the situation allows, this tip always gets me past the first 60 seconds of shallow breathing and the dreaded **blank nothing** moment.

✴ Things to Do: ACTION Mode for You

- Choose a "volunteer" from the group to help you demonstrate something, don't wait for someone to volunteer. Make sure that you are part of any demonstration with that volunteer.

- Just because the group is large does not mean that you have to remain on a stage in order to communicate. It's important for you to be in the midst of the action to get a feel for what the group is experiencing. Stand on a chair if needs be, but remain physically immersed in the process. Stay at least ten feet away from the insidious magnetic effect of the lectern.

☀ Things to Say and How to Say It

- Personalize what's going on by relating humorous historical moments that pertain to the task being attempted. "Do you know how *The Pamper Pole* got its name?" People like hearing about the history of an activity. Be true to what you know, but don't hesitate to embellish a bit.

- Announce that "world records are apt to tumble today." Talk about positive competition and how that relates to competing against their own best time or their last best effort, i.e. their recently established "world record."

- Be a cheerleader not a coach. If you have a clipboard, leave it home. Don't use a whistle to get their attention.

- I assume this is obvious, but... If you are in the middle of a large circled group, keep turning as you talk, or better yet, remain part of the circle's arc until you have said what you need to say

- If the group numbers over sixty participants, (varies as to how well you project your voice) use a lavelier mike. If the group swells to over one-hundred, don't think about it, use it. Hand or floor mikes are not as convenient because your movement will be restricted.

- Be "casually competent" in what you say and do. Your audience needs to know that you know what you're talking about. Be aware that casual competence is not casually acquired.

- Don't be predictable in what you say or do. Say strange things, ("Pair up by threes. Face each other back to back."). Perform a few out of context Tai-Chi movements when the class is involved in something else. Keep the anticipation level high and the predictability level low.

✳ And...

■ Choose activities that allow everyone to participate. If you want the really BIG response, everyone should be doing, trying, and accomplishing the same thing, i.e. operating as a TEAM. *Jumping Jack Flash* is a good example of an activity that allows everyone in a large group (100+) to feel a sense of team accomplishment.

■ At some point in your presentation (whether one hour or a full day) sit the group down and share a few words about processing/debriefing. Games and initiatives, particularly if things are going well, have a tendency to flow one to the next in a potpourri of play and high energy sharing. Undeniably fun, but there's more to adventure/experiential education than just activity and recreation: fear, delight, introspection, denial, joy, personal growth, anger, frustration, occupational epiphanies...talk about it.

■ The old vaudeville adage, "Leave 'em laughing" also applies to a day on the ropes course, or an afternoon of playing games. Don't just head 'em toward the bus. Finish up with something short, humorous, meaningful and pleasantly remembrable. Ex's. *The Spiral, PDQ, Yurt Rope, Perfect Circle*

✳ Sequencing

I have tried to sequence the activities in this book from introduction to wrap up. Some of the games are obviously best used as ice breakers and as an introduction to what's next. Some can be used practically anywhere, and some are designed as winder-uppers. Rather than flag each activity as to their "proper" sequence use, I'm going to start with those that seem to best fit at the beginning of a program and end with those that have a sense of finality. All the rest make up the bulk of the book.

✳ Processing the Large Group

Should you take the time and energy to process with a large group? Is it worth your or their time considering that, in most cases, participants don't have the chance to express personal comments? Does "large group" necessarily define the experience?

If you are offering adventure games, doing a few initiative problems, and asking the group to participate in a couple trust activities, I'm convinced that most of the time good things will happen within a large, or small group by educational osmosis (experiential collateral learning). However, considering GOOD as the first quality step of the GOOD/BETTER/BEST triumvirate, the better/best duo, as associated with total program quality, can only be achieved by taking the time and applying the soft skills associated with processing/debriefing/reviewing.

Gloree Rohnke, has been a trainer in the adventure education field for many years. A generalist by nature, she melds her experience in adventure-based programming, academics, counseling, and community prevention in her work. Gloree's recently developed adventure-based curriculums in asset development are currently being implemented in select New England school mentoring programs.

To encourage readers to expand their "bag of tricks," Gloree takes a fresh look at how the experiential reflection/review process can apply to large groups. She offers valuable insights and a number of hands-on techniques that allow a seamless segue from theory to practice. (See pages 63–79).

✳ Finally...

I've talked with, and at, a lot of teachers over the years, enough to know that professional pedagogues will use a selected activity exactly where they want to use it, so, in keeping with Harry Truman's suggestion of how to motivate young people, "Find out what they want to do, then suggest that they do it." Find out what the individuals in your group want and/or need and "suggest that they do it." If your suggestions are ignored, try benign subversion; let the program sell itself. Fortunately, it takes a fairly high level of incompetence to ruin a good activity.

The following games, initiative activities, and stunts are ones that I regularly use when I am asked to present at a conference session, corporate outing, or teacher in-service, particularly when the group numbers more than thirty.

What do I mean when I say "large group?" More than thirty, as just above? Yes, but certainly more than that also. For the purpose of this book and your needs I'd say "large" means over 30 and less than 75, but groups over 100, or 200, or even more, can have functional fun with these activities.

Limitations include; your own comfort level with large groups, the venue, the group itself (kindergarten, adjudicated, corporate, middle school) and your ability to project. Use a sound system when your vocal projection system has reached its limit.

The following anthology of games and initiatives are not just a collection of easily reproduced activities that fulfill the advertising. I use these activities on a regular basis. Some of them I made up, some were borrowed, some benignly purloined, but none have remained untouched or unchanged over the years. Every time I play a game or present an initiative problem, particularly with large groups, I'm always looking for that subtle phrase or change of presentation that's going to make it a better activity. I suggest you do the same. Become a game tweaker, it's empowering and functional. ...and think of the T-shirt possibilities: I Tweak for a living. Tweakers do it best. Tweak or Stagnate.

Caveat — Don't tweak commercial board game rules unless:

- All players are sympathetic and understanding of your penchant for game change (not likely).
- The players regularly quote passages from *Calvin and Hobbes*.
- You are single.

Introduction

The following activities are included in this book for two reasons:

1. I use them on a regular basis for conference presentations, in-service days, contracted game days, and adventure workshop settings; they are my favorites and they "work."

2. They function particularly well with large groups.

What's considered to be a large group? That depends on the experience and skill base of the facilitator, but for the purposes of this book let's set the operational perimeters at between 30 and 75 people. The activities below will certainly function as well, if not better, with 15 participants and with a decent speaker system some of the games would be well received by over 1,000 players.

What "works" does not depend so much on the size of the group or the activity chosen, as the skill and perceptiveness of the presenter. But, having said that, some games and initiatives seem to be better received by larger groups.

Within each activity write up, **bold print (like this), is me talking to you about game details, caveats, things to tweak, humorous asides, etc.** Regular print (like this), indicates straight forward expository text.

Panic Pages

These ten paragraphs alone could be worth the cost of this book.

> *"Hey, <u>insert your first name</u>, I need you to take that group tomorrow from International Chicken Products. There's about 75 coming for a couple hours. We need an ongoing training contract with this company, so show 'em what we can do."*

Here's what I would *do* with 75 uninitiated, divergent personalities for "a couple hours."

They show up. A corporate group usually arrives in separate vehicles. Have coffee ready and a few sugar-heavy, carbo treats. Some of the *Prevention Magazine* readers will want bagels, bottled water, or real juice. Don't be fancy, but don't skimp. If it's a group of young people, hold the coffee, try to limit the sugar loading, and collect their already completed liability forms from home.

- Mingle. Let them know that you are *their* person for the morning without announcing it.

- Do not let anyone wander around wondering what's going on.

- Pass out liability forms without a lot of discussion. Indicate that these forms are *necessary* for liability reasons; no equivocating, no excuses. If someone refuses to sign, that's liability-by-choice. Politely indicate to that person that they can observe but cannot participate. Have abundant pencils/pens available for this task and enough pieces of cardboard/clip-boards to write on.

■ Talk to people. Make comments about the day, their arrival, sport's teams, what's hot, what's not. They need to hear your voice and know that you are OK, i.e. within their realm of initial acceptance.

■ Start on time.

■ Ask everyone to join you somewhere other than where you have been drinking beverages, signing forms, etc. Change their venue, even if that means just walking a few yards to a new location.

Stand in front of the clustered group. (You don't have to start with a circle just because they expect to be in one.) Keep the sun or glare in *your* face. Do not wear sunglasses, they need to see your eyes. Ask them to come closer because, everyone always gives the presenter too much space, you won't have to talk as loudly, and it's friendlier. With animation (move your hands, head, body), briefly explain (2-3 minutes max) what you have in mind for the next couple of hours: hands-on participation, challenge by choice, experiential everything, funn...

Explain that you are going to demonstrate something unique, i.e. an esoteric movement or skill they may have vicariously experienced on TV, but never had the opportunity to try. Demonstrate something *you can do* that is unique (a dance step, a karate move, a Tai-Chi movement). Your plan is to encourage the group to all try something new, something unfamiliar, recognizing that it can be the attempt, not the performance level or completion that's satisfying.

Try to choose a movement that can be shared. For example, demonstrate a simple dance step. (See *Heel Clicker*, page 3.)

After a few klutzy tries by everyone, and more than one out-burst of laughter, pairs can attempt the step together, then perhaps as a trio, or even a performing quad. Encourage humor, recognizing that failure in this context can be simply that moment of enjoyable hesitation before the next attempt. Will attempting to learn this dance step pragmatically help anyone occupationally? Probably not, but the acceptance of trying something new in a supportive atmosphere can have profound transference implications within the work place or at school.

Looking for further rationale to fend off the inevitable *Why?* questions from parents or administrators. Emphasize the old stand-byes of, building communication (talking and listening), cooperating, establishing a level of trust, learning how to fail forward, experiencing unselfconscious touch, establishing self concept...

Don't forget to occasionally make time for questions and/or discussion about what's been going on. You mean like having fun? Sure, but what about, when, where, why, who, then what? Hey, there's more to this than I thought. Gotcha!

Disclaimer

Please use caution and venue awareness while attempting to play and or present the games and initiatives included in *Small Book...* Life obviously involves some risk, however, risk for the sake of risk is not conducive to continued good health or the achievement of your curriculum goals.

The reader assumes all risk and liability for any loss or damage which may result from the use of materials contained within this book. Liability for any claim, whether based upon errors or omisions in this book shall be limited in amount to the purchase price.

Over Twenty of My Favorite Large Group Activities

Share-a-Stretch

Most of the time I find myself presenting to adult groups. We (that's the royal WE) aren't as young and limber as we used to be, so I often ask the group to join me in a shared stretch. I'm sure most of the participants interpret the stretching as something I include to prevent injury, but that's not my rationale for using the first few minutes to "bend and touch your toes."

Admittedly, I do make a couple ease-the-angst statements about "not being as young as we used to be," or ask "everyone above the age of fifteen to join me." But that's just for easing and teasing; ease any fear of participating in real exercise, and tease out a smile or two.

I ask the participants to visualize their favorite anatomical stretch, something they might personally include before exercising, and begin doing it. With almost every participant doing something that looks halfway healthy, I suggest that everyone look around (keep stretching) to see what everyone else is doing, then copy any stretch that looks useful, comfortable, or interesting. Continue this look-and-do sharing until everyone has tried 2-3 different stretching motions.

If not for prevention of injury or increased health benefits, what's going on? In a nut shell, copying a movement fosters immediate sharing and also subtly encourages each person to try something new.

As facilitator, join the varied stretching movements, calling out words of encouragement, overtly laughing, and occasionally pointing out a particularly interesting or bizarre stretch. It's also a time for you to enjoy the sharing, the inevitable glib comments, and bizarre contortions that are "out of text."

If you have done much stretching, you probably know that stretching is done most effectively *after* exercise. Since you are asking the group to stretch *before* exercise, don't get too

serious about the amplitude or speed of the movements, i.e. don't get hurt.

I seldom use this "exercise" ploy with younger groups, admittedly playing on an adult's need to initially DO something adult-like and recognizable. Younger groups also respond well to initial physical movement, but the activities don't need to be as traditional; *Hog Call* for example.

✳ Variation

Share-a-Scar is an ice breaker activity that encourages participants to share information about small personal scars. (Hold the emotional scars!) **Have players pair up and spend a couple minutes informing their newly discovered confidant about "...how they hit a car bumper and got six stitches while sledding on a dirt road back in 19??... and how come we don't have fun like that anymore?"**

Bring the pairs back together after about five minutes and ask if anyone would like to share what they learned about their partner, adhering to the precept of Scar-by-Choice, of course. If your group numbers over 30, limit the sharing to no more than fifteen minutes. Scars are fun to hear about, for maybe sixteen minutes.

Heel Clicker

I particularly like this participation gambit because the entire activity sequence is based on one simple dance movement. Also, the size of the group is only limited by the participation area of the venue.

Tell the group you are going to demonstrate a dance step, and that you would like them to try and duplicate the movement. Before you begin, assure the players of being more interested in their honest attempt than how well they "cut a rug."

The success of your demonstration obviously depends entirely upon your ability to "do" this dance step, called a *Heel Clicker* (Ref. Gene Kelly in the movie *Singing in the Rain*). You certainly don't need to perform like Gene Kelly, but you should be able to click your heels together passingly well so the participants have a move to emulate. If you don't know how to click your heels, find some other physical movement that you do well to use as a give-this-a-try demonstration. Various dance steps serve this purpose because they represent something that most people have vicariously observed but rarely tried. The crux of this exercise is to try something new without fear of censure or ridicule.

In case you're interested in clicking your heels (a stylized "jump for joy"), here's how. Encourage laughter in all these activities—laughter *with*, rather than laughter *at*, particularly when you are demonstrating.

- Stand with all your weight on your right leg with your left leg held straight off to the side, left foot about 12" off the floor.

- Jump straight up on the right leg, then quickly kick the heel of the right foot against the heel of the left foot. Land on the right foot.

- Crow hop from the right leg to the left leg. The right foot is now about 12" off the floor.

- Repeat bullet #2, except using opposite legs.

- Continue this heel kicking (clicking) action from side to side; get into the flow.

If you were convincing enough, everyone should now be attempting a heel click or two, sharing merriment and mirth, but hopefully not a heel in the shins. Praise the various attempts. Offer private (albeit short) lessons. Encourage, cajole, wheedle, smile a lot, chuckle often. **Encourage multiple attempts, letting your players find out, via experience, that looking good is not as important as experiencing fun and the satisfaction of trying something new in a supportive atmosphere. Be patient. Remember, these people have been trained by society (in its various restrictive forms) to be cool, and to never attempt something in public that might make them appear less than cool.**

Choose some smiling person as a "volunteer." Ask that person to hold your hand, and do the heel-clicker movement with you, performing as a dancing duo. **From your subtle preactivity observations, pick someone who you think isn't going to stumble or kick you in the shins.** After your convincing duo demonstration (thank your dashing and daring partner), ask each person to give the heel-clicker motion a try with their own partner. Let the action and observation continue for 60 seconds or so, all the while continuing your reinforcing patter and overwhelming interest in whatever they accomplish.

Ask each "highly successful" pair to introduce themselves to another pair and try doing some lateral heel clicking as a quad. **By this time the energy level's up, most recognizing that quality kicking is not #1, and that the social aspect of doing something you don't do well, with others of the same affliction, is not only acceptable but downright attractive.**

Continue the kicking routine with eight participants, then sixteen if you have enough people in the group. Eventually (don't rush to a finale) ask everyone to make a large circle around you and join hands for a June Taylor-like, heel clicking extravaganza. Let the group plan and implement their own final performance, (partners, direction, timing). When the rhythmical kicking begins, let it go until *they* want it to stop. Look for: grasping, gasping, holding, kicking, stumbling, laughing, shouting, applauding, enormous smiles, lots of teeth, happy.

Total time from your initial demonstration to the circular finale above - about 10 minutes.

For a young group, *Heel Clicker* might be too initially intimidating. Build the trust level between participants, and the trust they have in you as leader, before suggesting a hand holding "dance" commitment.

Sometimes, after a successful heel clicking routine, I'll start talking about other dance steps and mention how physically demanding ballet can be. Segue to an *entrechat* (a balletic gymnastic-like jump indigenous to the dance), or perhaps a demo of the five basic ballet positions. If you can't remember the stylistic moves, there's *always* someone in the group who can't wait to show you.

Potential participants are willing to try even complex esoteric movements or sequences as long as they feel part of a supportive group that is enjoying the action together.

Gotcha

Over the years, *Gotcha* has become a well used opening gambit/ice breaker for use with large groups. Its one drawback is its popularity; the activity *Gotcha* is no longer unique. But every time I assume a certain activity is well known, I get blank stares when I mention the game's name. Anyway, *Gotcha's* good for multiple attempts. Enjoy the play.

Standing in a circle, ask everyone in the arc to hold their right hand, palm up, with their right elbow bent at about a 90° angle. Take the left hand, with index finger extended, and place the tip of that rigid digit into the offered palm of the person to their left. **Check it out, everybody has one palm and one index finger involved, very friendly.**

On a signal, the extended palms try to catch a finger, and obviously the rigid digits try to escape. (This is a one move game. If a finger isn't grabbed immediately, that's it, no second grabs.) Individually, if you can both capture a finger and also escape capture you have achieved to the premier level of Gotcha Gamesmanship. But don't get too steamed up over your newly acquired status, there's another attempt coming up. **Give the first couple signals to Go!, then back off and allow one of the players to initiate the *Gotcha* sequence. See variation below.**

Half a dozen attempts are enough to achieve your ice breaking, come-join-in facilitating goals. Don't get suckered in by the group's enthusiasm, thinking that *Gotcha* is THE game for all time. It *is* a great activity to coax hesitant players to take a chance and have some fun, but after 6-8 attempts it can become as tedious as any game played too often and too long.

If your circle becomes unmanageably large (like in a small indoor space), *Gotcha* can be made more manageable if you:

- **Ask everyone to count off, 1-2 all the way around the circle.**
- **Have the ones take a step forward and do an about face so that you have two concentric circles with everyone facing one another. With alternating palms and fingers at the ready, it's then easy to arrange a unique via-á-vis *Gotcha* set up.**

☀ Variations

- Turn the receiving palm upside down (palm faces the ground). That means the extended digit now comes from the bottom up. Not a biggie, but well received nonetheless.
- Choose someone in the group to say Go! by indicating something that identifies that person. Ex. Anyone in the group from Arizona..., anyone in the group with red socks on..., etc. **Consider your question carefully**

before asking it. Remember, "thoughts can become words at any time."

- Have everyone close their eyes and indicate that anyone can give the signal after five seconds, which will be the shortest five seconds imaginable.

This is a **FUNN**, (Functional Understanding's Not Necessary) activity as presented, i.e. play for the sake of play, hoping that people will join in and become part of the participating group. Verbally dissecting this particular activity seems contraindicated toward what you are trying to achieve.

*"Dissecting fun is like dissecting a frog,
you may learn more about the frog,
but you kill it in the process."*

Galloping Hands

You will need folding chairs, one per person. Actually you could sit on the turf, or carpet, or floor, but I like the way a chair causes your rectus femoris muscle to align itself for solid hand contact (more on that).

I have introduced *Galloping Hands* to over one-hundred seated players with good results, but I don't think I'd want many more than that.

Circle up the chairs so that each person is sitting directly next to the person sitting next to them, i.e. close. Place your hands, palms down, on the upper part of your leg (distal to the rectus femoris, as above). Demonstrate a substantial spanking motion with semi-cupped palms to produce a distinct slapping sound on both legs. Invite the group to join you, emphasizing a quality slapping sound, remembering, when you try to do the ridiculous well, good things usually happen.

After having displayed that they can and will slap with abandon **(you may not have recognized it, but joining you in that frenzied group-leg-abuse required a fairly high level of trust; trust in you and trust you were not leading them toward total embarrassment)**, suggest that they follow a 1-2 slap sequence starting with you and continuing all the way around the circle. If you decide to move clockwise with the slap sequence it would be your right hand, then left hand (slap, slap), then the right hand of the person to your left (slap), then that person's left hand (slap), etc.

Praise the group for completing a round, then ask for another circle slap, this time increasing the speed of the slap wave. *You* **are making this happen. Without your verbal support and cheer leader-like enthusiasm it's over; don't stop the patter.** By this time they should be operating in a speed mode, however, still not recognizing where the accelerator's located. Comment about the staccato slap-slap sequence, encouraging them to "break it down and find the flow." Encourage a few more incrementally faster circuits, gradually abandoning themselves to the flow.

After a round of self applause for going "faster than any other group you have been with all day," suggest that each person develop an in-brain sound for speed, and for each person to play it back within the confines of their cranium, i.e. silent on the exterior. On the count of three, ask everyone to loudly vocalize their, as yet, unexpressed sound. Having done this en masse, asking individuals to combine the sound and hand movement won't seem so embarrassing. Every time it's their turn to slap/slap, as part of the developing speed sequence, the addition of their speed sound may help—can't hurt.

After a few more hand slap rotations, including starts, stops and reverses, announce that it's time for some head-to-head, hard core competition. Indicate you will start the hand slap again, but this time sending it clockwise and counterclockwise simultaneously via Team A and Team B. **Look to your right and designate that seated person as captain of Team A, then look immediately to your left and say "Howdy" to the Team B captain.** Obviously when the slapping movements meet one another (far side of the circle), the head-on hand slap impulses must existentially move through one another and continue on back toward the finish, i.e. YOU, the initiator. First impulse back obviously wins. **Did you understand that? Good, it was meant to engender obfuscation, because if you really tried to make sense of impulses passing through one another, a quantum jump to paradigm shifts would, of necessity, reverse the group's polarity. That's a paranickel observation by the way, (half a paradigm!).**

Essentially then, when you're playing, knowing *why* isn't nearly as important as knowing *how*. OK, but who wins, Team A or Team B? I mean, is the winner the team that starts the impulse or the team that brings it home? If this often heard query doesn't humorously initiate a discussion about the vagaries of competition, you're taking me in context. Be a catalyst, make things happen.

Competition is a loaded concept with heated opinions available at both ends of the win/lose spectrum and everywhere in between. A discussion is supposed to reveal new information, not necessarily change opinions. Don't let the discussion become an argument; facilitate joyfully.

Competition Topics

Positive competition — When the competition is against self, time, or a "team" from Western Wherever.

Negative competition — Competition that produces a loser.

※ The Competition Pyramid (according to Karl)

▦   **At the apex of the pyramid are the varsity athletes, those people who deserve to be at the top because: ...of their genetic make up ...their dedication to the activity ...a high tolerance for repetition and long practice sessions ...their desire to be the best and to win.**

▦   **At the next level, the junior varsity; those competitors who meet all the criteria above but either haven't put in their time, or fall short in the skill or natural talent area. By definition there are more J.V. players than Varsity athletes.**

▦   **The next level of participant does not have a title or designation other than what the activity provides. Players here are those who enjoy occasional competitive get togethers; weekend warriors, senior teams at school, intramurals, club teams... There are quite a few of these players.**

▦   **The next few levels of participation are indistinct, almost blending into one another, but bottoming out with people who don't participate at any level because they don't have the skills, coordination, body morphology or inclination to compete at what have become unrealistic levels. That's not to say that these** people don't enjoy participating at some peer competition level, but how has society provided for the majority of these players at the base of the pyramid? Interactive TV! (Wear your team's jersey.) Cheering on the "varsity" heroes. (How many games can you watch on a Sunday?). Learning how to give a "high 5" while sitting down. (Shared camaraderie.)

The smallest number of participants (apex) play the most. The greatest number of players (base) play the least. How can we turn this pyramid upside down? Eliminating losers is a good start.

Hog Call

There's really no limit to the number of people you can involve in *Hog Call*, but practically (size of venue and post-activity sharing) I'd limit the group to 50-60.

Situation #1: **Beginning of a workshop, in service day, staff training, etc. Beau coup people have arrived, had their coffee/juice/bagel, and are standing alone or talking with friends. It's time for some large group action, it's time to be outrageous.** *Don't let these people think for a minute that this is going to be another sit-and-listen-to-me day.*

Situation #2: **First day of classes. Students are milling about, heads down, maybe talking with an acquaintance; appearing cool and unaffected is prime. Start this year off differently. Break some preconceptions, create some new contacts, set yourself up as different.** *Don't let these people think for a minute that this is going to be another sit-and-listen-to-me day.*

- Ask the participants to make one long line facing you, standing shoulder to shoulder.
- Ask the line to fold in half (double up into two lines) so that everyone is facing someone.
- Each person, face to face, should introduce themselves to their temporary partner, first names only. Emphasize remembering that one person's name.
- Ask one half of the line (group 1) to walk to one end of an open area (soccer pitch is ideal), and the other half (group 2) to walk to the opposite end. That's correct, partners end up at opposite ends of the field.
- A facilitator is with each group and offers the following instructions.

   1. In a minute you will be asked to close your eyes, then try to find your partner by voicing only his/her name.

   2. When you make contact with your partner, open your eyes and ask them; where they are from, why they are here, and what book or movie is their latest favorite?

   3. If you feel that you need to open your eyes (peek by choice), that's OK, as long as the peek doesn't help you find your partner.

   4. As you're walking and saying (shouting) your partner's name, keep your hands (palms out, elbows bent) extended in front of you at about chin level. This is called "bumpers up" and is meant to protect you and the people around you within this cacophony of voices. Ready, Go! Make sure you and some other responsible person protect the visually challenged participants as they make their well heard walk.

After correct contact is made and information is shared, ask all the participants to return together and sit in a circle. Pairs do not necessarily have to sit together. Introduction of partners are made, including whatever information sharing is comfortable. Let pairs volunteer when they want to make their introductions, and if a couple chooses not to share at that particular time, let it go.

This "game" obviously involves a loud medley of voices as participants attempt to shout loud enough for their partner to hear them. If you are in an area where noise would be disruptive (conference setting) indicate that everyone must whisper their partner's name. The name of the game is obviously *Hog Whisper*. Certainly you have heard of a Horse Whisperer. This is the same kind of thing, except with a hog.

※ Why Hog Call?

- All you have to do is remember one name.

- It's hard to be embarrassed when everyone is doing the same off-the-wall thing you are doing. The game engenders trust and underlines the concept that Adventure/Experiential Education depends upon the concept of shared stupidity.

- *Hog Call* is a dandy way to handle group introductions and find out a few personal things about the people with whom you will be sharing time, learning, and emotion.

- The game is just bizarre enough to stimulate interest without causing disaffection.

- People (particularly adults) don't realize how much fun it is (was) to yell, until they are yelling.

- *Projected Proverbs* and *Hog Call* are both games requiring commitment to generate a large amount of personal noise. *Projected Proverbs* is more adult task oriented, *Hog Call* is a younger person's ice breaker and get-to-know-you game.

jected Proverbs

Fifty or sixty players might be the upper limit for this noisy activity, but if 75 show up, I'd give it a try.

Standing in a circle, ask each person to look to their immediate right and left in order to get a real good look at the person standing on either side, (who's probably looking the other way; be patient.) Don't give any indication as to why, just emphasize a detailed visual examination of those two people. Talking is allowed, initiating considerable nervous chatter amidst the sharing.

Then ask each person to come up with a favorite proverb (aphorism, same thing). If they can't think of a proverb, (Ex. *It's a long lane that has no turning. A bird in the hand...*) a simple phrase will do, (I like beans and hot dogs). Indicate that they should repeat their chosen proverb/phrase to the person on their right and left, the same two people that you asked them to look at closely. Indicate that it's OK for anyone to hear what's being said, it's not a secret. Ask each person to clearly verbalize their proverb a second time, and maybe even a third. **During this prep time you have still not given any indication as to the nature of the challenge. Be definitive, interested and convincing as you make these pregame requests. They need to know you really want them to concentrate on just these two simple tasks, strongly hinting that there is an imminent performance rationale for which they are preparing.**

Explain what bumpers up* means, assume that position, then ask everyone to close their eyes and mill around slowly for 20 seconds or so. **During that sightless twenty seconds keep up a steady supportive patter, just so they know you are still there and concerned about their well being.** When the group appears mixed and separated, ask them to stop, keep their eyes closed, and listen to you for an explanation of the challenge.

Before outlining the task, make a few supportive comments about participating with their eyes closed toward establishing a workable student/instructor level of trust. Assure everyone you will not do anything that would cause embarrassment, and that you will do your best to maintain the safety of each person. Indicate that if anything occurs that appears beyond your ability to protect any one person, you will shout the word *STOP*. On hearing your shout, everyone should immediately stop where they are and open their eyes. If operating for a few minutes with their eyes closed troubles anyone to the extent that they need to see where they are and what's happening, they should avail themselves of the opportunity to "peek by choice," but certainly not allow that brief peek to help them solve the problem.

The Problem

Operating without sight, try to reestablish the people circle as it was originally formed. The only thing they are allowed to verbalize during this sightless search is their chosen proverb, usually "projected" with some volume. I think you will be impressed (and so will they) at the accuracy resulting from their proverbial din.

After the circle is intact and the inevitable post-blindfold flood of words has slowed, encourage the circled folks to share their individual proverb. Some are funny, some touching, some profound, with the occasional arcane reference to the incomprehensible.

Bumpers Up — Hands are held up at face level, palms forward with elbows bent. A self-protective position assumed when people are moving slowly with their eyes closed.

Pairs Tag

If I had to pick an ideal number of participants to play *Pairs Tag*, it would be in the 30-40 category. Not a large, large group game, but large enough to qualify for some fun and function.

People like *Pairs Tag* because "it moves." Reading about the game without the requisite bodies to make it happen will surely convince a reader that this author has precious little insight into what makes a good game. Trust me reader, this is a good game for small and large groups.

Mark out a boundary* line for *Pairs Tag* using the basketball lines on a court or, on a field, casually arrange a retired climbing rope as an outline. (There is a commercial product available called *Lawn Staples* that allows "stapling" rope to the turf in whatever configuration fits your game needs. How about *Pairs Tag* inside a rhombus?) Choosing game boundaries requires some experience, but basically the smaller the boundary, the better the game. For 20 people I'd choose an area measuring approximately 40' X 40'. There are no official boundary dimensions for *Pairs Tag* because this is not an official game. And since "official" is not part of the game description, there is no time limit, no winners (or losers), or even rules; just three safety considerations, and they are as follows.

■ Inadvertent physical contact with other players is going to happen. When it happens, emphasize compassionate contact. This is not just a rule, it is a mantra for this game.

- ■ **No head tags.**
- ■ **Walking only. Does that mean** *No Running*? **Exactly correct.**

Now that you are imbued with the non-rules, here's what you are trying to accomplish while *Pairs Tag* is unofficially being played. Like in any tag game, you will be trying to tag your partner, and in so doing, establishing that person as IT. In a nut shell: You're IT. Chase your partner and tag them, then get away before you're tagged.

That's it, that's the whole game. Give the group a quick demo with you and a volunteer trading tags. Tag back and forth a couple times to demonstrate the huge potential for fun. **By this time the group may be looking at you like a pack of RCA radio dogs, wondering not only where you're coming from, but hoping you go there.**

Do whatever you do to pair up the group. Use the line technique, as in *Hog Call* above, or count off 1,2-1,2... around the circle. Indicate that the tallest person of the pair is IT (or the shortest, or the one with the longest hair...), and for that person to remain stationary as the person to be chased moves away. While this distancing is taking place, reinforce the concept of trying to stay within the exceptionally small play area, no head tags, walk only, and GO!

Within less than five seconds the Ho-hum attitude is history as people shuck and jive trying to find and/or tag their "Pairs" partner. The restricted play area practically demands restricted movement, constant body contact, and unrestrained smiles. Check it out.

Allow the action to unfold and swirl for about two minutes with you in the center of the action as a permanent "pick," a benignly battered, but persistent obstacle. When the action

slows, yell out they have ten seconds left to play and, "Don't be the last one caught." There is no consequence for being the last IT, but a frantic increase in movement belies the fact.

People respond well to this game, I believe, because the rules are few, atypical, and simple. Also the action is constant, there is an unspoken sensation of risk, and the personal involvement is total.

Be aware that aggressive people can drastically change the game and what you are trying to accomplish. Stop the game immediately if you see "playground" or "recess" rules being used, and use the break to review the purpose for playing *Pairs Tag*. (Maybe it's time to talk about the function of games, play and fun.) Fun? Absolutely. Try to find out how the players define or identify fun. "We had fun last night breaking windows!" No, no, no...

✳ Variations

- Suggest having pairs chasing pairs utilizing the same game format as above. You might want to extend the boundaries a bit for the expanded action (see *boundary** below)

- Revert back to a single pair. Each person in the game puts their semi-closed fist up to their eye, allowing a restricted tunnel vision view of the people, action, and play area. Play as above, but remind the players to move slowly and utilize their free hand to tag and act as a bumper. Keep both eyes and your safety sensors on alert, as this variation, combined with unbounded enthusiasm, can sideline safety.

*Boundary — After the students have played a few games where boundaries are involved, I remove the physical boundaries announcing, "The fun takes place here." In other words, play and fun occur where other people are most closely collected. You may be "safe" over there, but being safe (untaggable) in the context of this game isn't much fun.

> *"I was never good at hide and seek because*
> *I'd always make enough noise so my friends*
> *would be sure to find me. I don't have anyone to*
> *play those games with me anymore, but now and*
> *then I make enough noise just in case someone*
> *is still looking and hasn't found me yet."*
> Brian Andreas

Everybody's IT

The classic counter-culture tag game that can be played effectively with almost any sized group. Twenty people playing? Everybody's IT! One-hundred people playing? Everybody's still IT! It's true.

When I was a kid, you either liked or disliked tag games. If you were a fast runner, tag games were great fun. If you were slow (for whatever reason) tag was a drag. *Everybody's It*, particularly when played in a restricted area, works for most everyone. Slow runners are still going to get caught, but there's some room for craftiness and guile. Also, getting caught is basically a rest position, immediately and visually shared by many other players; not a bad position all-in-all.

✳ Rules

- Everyone is IT, and tries to tag every other player. No head tags.
- When you're tagged, kneel down to prevent multiple tags.
- Last one caught breathes the hardest. Start another game.

If a game lasts for more than 2 minutes, something's wrong. Either gang up on the fastest runner, or introduce the no-back-up rule, which states: "when two runners confront one another face-to-face, the first runner to initiate a backward (retreating) movement is automatically caught." You're the ref, do your thing.

This game has to do with choice. If an adept person wants to run-run-run, the game allows that level of activity. If a non-runner, or a person who is feeling mellow wants to cool it, or

simply be an observer, all they have to do is kneel down. Who's to know? Who's to care?

A session of *Everybody's It* lasts for about a minute. So, with people choosing their level of commitment to the game, and considering the short time span, this is an ideal activity to use as a warm up for whatever curriculum gem you have in mind to follow.

Caveat — *Everybody's It*, despite it's initial "funn" potential, can easily become disliked if overplayed. It's a good warm up activity; it's deadly as a 3-day-in-a-row curricular choice. Ref. floor hockey, kick ball, murder ball.

Up Chuck

Up Chuck is a very simple and useful game. You need one soft throwable item per participant, e.g. fleece or Nerf ball. Do not use tennis balls, they hurt. If your program can afford the throwable objects, this game is applicable to almost any size group.

☀ Rules

- Anybody can stand anywhere.
- On a signal, all throwables are to be lofted *simultaneously* to a minimum height of 12 feet. There is no maximum height limit.
- Each player tries to catch a ball they did not throw.
- Multiple balls can be caught.
- Catches on the bounce do not count.

The object is to determine, as a team, (everybody's on the same team) how many balls can be caught per throw. Announce that unlimited attempts can be made. The attempts cease when the group is satisfied (or fed up) with what they have accomplished. **Remember, it is not your role as facilitator to judge their attempts, rather to act as a catalyst to encourage additional attempts and interact.**

After a throw, ask everyone who caught a ball to hold it up over their head for a team count. **Eventually it becomes easier, and less time consuming, to just count the balls missed, but people like to display their catching prowess, and no one likes to admit they missed, so take the time to count the catches. Check out the smiling catchers versus all the half smiling droppers. See what I mean?**

Up Chuck looks a lot like the game *Phones and Faxes* (*Silver Bullets*, page 63), but they are quite different. Both activities allow great visuals and photographs for your brochure.

Cutey a.k.a. QT a.k.a. Quick Touch

In a large group (30-300), ask lots of people to turn toward someone else and touch that person quickly (and appropriately). You have just asked a group of strangers to revisit a time honored tag movement; simple, engaging, some risk, entertaining, engenders smiles. Did you touch me? No, I tagged you.

Demonstrate that same quick touch (tag) with a chosen volunteer and ask them to respond in kind. Explain the no-head-touch rule (keeping fingers away from eyes). Also explain what *appropriate touch* means. Then ask for the pairs to expand the single touch (tag) they made earlier into a growing frenzy of tag-backs, until it's obvious that they not only remember what TAG was like, but look like they are enjoying it. **People like this introduction to TAG because there is no running (chasing), no embarrassment, and the encounter lasts only about 15 seconds.**

Now ask the group to drop the partner routine and try to tag as many other people as they can, at the same time trying to keep from being tagged. Rapid lateral movement and pivoting is obviously allowed but running or even walking is discouraged. A couple steps in any direction should bring you close enough to a lot of other maneuvering bodies to provide lots of tagging targets, (look out behind you!) There is no consequence for being tagged.

A frenetic tagging scene ensues, let it happen. Call a halt to the action after 20-30 seconds and (when you can talk with-

out gasping) ask if they can think of a single word to describe what they all just experienced. The word *PLAY* comes to mind, defined as fun; wildly competitive, no winners or losers, risky, enjoyable, no rationale for participation, no teams, no coaches, and coupled with copious laughter. Rhetorically ask, "When was the last time you played?" Something to think about as an adult.

Having practiced and developed a tolerable quick touch, introduce this timed initiative that will test the group's newly tolerated hands-on inclination. The challenge: Pass a touch through the entire group (person to person, i.e. sequentially) as quickly and efficiently as possible so that the touch starts with one person and ends with another.

✳ Rules

- ▦ It must be a sequentially passed touch, not an impulse. An impulse is described as a squeeze rather than the movement required of a touch.
- ▦ Each person in the group must be touched as part of the sequence.
- ▦ The touch can be started in one direction only.
- ▦ How a group arranges their sequence is up to the group.
- ▦ A stop watch accurate to the nearest 100th of a second is obviously necessary to meet NST (National Speed Touch) requirements.

Some people in the group will try their best to think their way out of the problem. This can be interpreted most favorably as thinking out-of-the box, or more realistically as attempting to circumvent the challenge by being crafty (sneaky). Present the challenge unequivocally. There is a difference between creative thinking and exploiting a travesty.

You are there to maintain the integrity of the challenge, at the same time supporting truly creative thinking, often a fine line.

There are techniques that allow lowering participation time, with a group of 50 participants, from about thirty seconds to less than two seconds. Considering that this is possible, recognize that IT IS NOT YOUR ROLE TO EVALUATE A GROUP'S SUCCESS. If a group is happy with their well deserved result (whatever it happens to be), do not deflate their achievement by mentioning that, "you did pretty good, but last week there was a group that..."

You're interested in the 2 second ploy, right? Can't blame you, I would be too. The group stands in two lines facing one another with one hand extended. The hands need to be very close to one another but not touching, (this might necessitate standing sideways). On GO!, a person at one end of the double line initiates a shove to the domino oriented hands resulting in a final time of two seconds or less. DO NOT give away this idea to a group; let it happen or not happen. You are NOT there to provide answers.

Weird Walking

I almost always present *Weird Walking* in a gymnasium or a conference ball room, so the venue limits the group size to about one-hundred. Outside, on a soccer pitch, I'd go for at least 150!

A Monty Python skit called *The Ministry of Silly Walks* was the impetus for this large group event. "Large" in this case is limited to the size of the venue and how well you can project your voice.

Ask your group to make a flanking line (shoulder to shoulder) facing you. Standing on one of the basketball sidelines works okay, as does using the sideline of a football or soccer field, or set out two parallel play ropes.

Indicate with some enthusiasm that you would like everyone in the line to move from where they are standing toward where you are standing, about ten yards distant. Encourage each individual to move across the open area (line to line) in some creative way. Indicate that the ten yard area is not *poison peanut butter* or any other fabricated noxious substance, simply a welcoming, comfortable area to do their ambulatory thing.

Provide them with a demonstration; make the crossing yourself exhibiting some bizarre foot/leg movement. **Always be ready to either demonstrate or be part of the action. Adventure education is anathema to clipboard teaching; you must be ready, on a regular basis, to demonstrate whatever you intend to ask the students to try. Walk, hop, dance, wiggle, skip, roll, be different, be a role model for zany creativity.** Can they come across alone? Yes. Can they join with a partner? Soon, but not this time. Ready, GO!

Congratulate everyone profusely. Make supportive comments as the crossings are made. Draw positive attention to the silliest most creative attempts.

Ask the suddenly buzzing group to join with someone else (share a first name) and make the creative crossing as a pair, maintaining physical contact throughout. **More supportive comments. Laugh like you mean it, enjoy the moment.** If you are reading this and know that you would not enjoy this activity or adventure games of this sort, do not pursue becoming a games facilitator because your players will soon know that you don't like playing, and that's the end. But that's not the case, so...

Third time, collect two pairs together (don't forget names) and make the crossing as a creative quad. Suggest adding a sound if the quad thinks it's appropriate or adds to the fun. How about making the crossing with eight people? Is it OK to make the crossing with seven or nine? Sure. **See *Categories* below, second paragraph, for a game change at this juncture.**

The finale involves moving the entire group en masse. This might appear to be the easiest way to cross, but with discussion and decision making involved it may well prove to be the most time consuming. **Applaud whatever crossing arrangement is made, and include yourself if the time and situation seem right.**

This is not a profound activity that lends itself to an in depth debrief/review, but the adventure triumvirate of cooperation, communication and trust are heavily used and should be mentioned as essential aspects of working together to achieve a goal.

Final point — goals do not have to be reached to exhibit transference. Did the group make the final crossing in good form? It doesn't really matter. What does matter is that everyone worked together while making the attempt. Can they achieve this level of cooperation in another context? You can count on it.

Categories

I'm pretty sure I got this idea from the book *Playfair* by Joel Goodman and Matt Weinstein. I don't know of many other "quick hitters" like this coalescing gem; an activity, requiring no props, that captures so quickly a group's collective imagination and enthusiasm. But the real attraction for facilitators is the ease of application (no props) and immediate who-are-you results.

I often use the activity *Categories* as a vehicle for game change. For example; consider a group well into the activity *Weird Walking*, already sharing creative ideas and physical responses in order to make a bizarre and zany crossing of the gym floor. (See *Weird Walking* above.)

After the singles, pairs, then quad crossing has taken place, I ask the group to all fold their arms, as if waiting impatiently for something to happen. This request is completely out of context with what they had been attempting, so the confusion and curiosity factor is usually high. What's this guy doing now?

Indicate that all arm folders with their right arm folded on top should move to your right, and those with their left arm on top should move as quickly to your left. With a group of about 30-500+ you may be surprised how accurately the group has divided themselves in half.

Why? Other than the fact that arm folding is a genetic trait, I don't know. And you don't need to know either, just use the results to obtain what is now an approximate and predictable 50/50 split. Benefits? You are cast in the omniscient role of "knowing" wise and wonderful things, and you get a usable split without having to revert to the old sociogram technique of two best friends or two best athletes choosing up sides...and you know who's going to be chosen last...like always.

But folding arms is going to get old, fast. Too true, but here's the great part, there are numerous *categories* to use, and people like finding things out about themselves that are intrinsically useless but at the same time hugely fascinating. To wit:

■ Fold your hands. Which thumb is on top? Try putting the other thumb on top. Kinda weird, eh?

■ Have the group look at their finger nails and hold that position. Some will be looking at the back of an extended hand, the rest will be looking toward their palm with their fingers folded down. Why? Remember, it doesn't matter, just use the results, which in this case will be skewed toward those looking at the back of their hands. Why? See Why? above.

■ Take a look at your elbow. Which elbow did you look at?

■ Turn around. Did you turn clockwise or otherwise?

■ Pretend you are facing a ladder and about to climb. Which foot goes on the bottom rung?

■ With which eye do you wink?

■ When licking ice cream, do you rotate the cone clockwise or counterclockwise?

■ For a plethora (more than 20) of *Categories*, see the book *The Bottomless Bag Again!?* page 143.

You have segued into another activity without so much as a single word about what happened to *Weird Walking*. Now, use a category technique to get about a 50/50 split, and ask those two large groups to return to their weird walkin' ways and decide amongst themselves how they are going to make their crossing as two separate groups (physical contact and maybe some sound this time.) Finish up with the entire group moving creatively en masse.

From *Weird Walking* to *Categories* back to *Weird Walking* is an example of game change and sequencing that precludes the old do-this-then-we-do-that approach, all toward maintaining interest, building trust, and establishing a keen sense of anticipation.

The Dog Shake

***The Dog Shake* is different... real different. It's a zany and well received activity if sequenced for the right time and right place. Pulling it off requires a fairly high level of chutzpah from the leader (you).**

The Dog Shake is demonstrated (in slow motion) by you, indicating histrionically how a dog initiates the drying process after getting out of the water.

Initiate a slow shake by starting at your nose and head, then continuing the shake down your torso, pelvis, legs and finishing at your toes, so that at the end of the sequence your body is involved in total corporal shaking. **Quality of shaking is not so important; however, consistent patter and enthusiasm is key.**

The students will enjoy this solo demo immensely. Your task is to convince and cajole them into joining you for a joint second "shake."

This activity was not designed specifically for a large group, it just happens to work well with any size group. Actually, the more people the better. It's easier to participate, or lose yourself, as part of a large group.

Unless you are the guru of all facilitators (or preternaturally lucky), do not present *The Dog Shake* during your first meeting with your experiential group because:

- they probably have no idea what experiential means.
- they may split as you begin your otherworldly demonstration.
- zany does not play well with uninitiated people.

Practice *The Dog Shake* (after having seen it demonstrated) in front of a mirror, in your bathroom, with the door closed. Practice it more than once. Present the activity with gusto and enthusiasm throughout.

✳ Why Shake?

- It gives the students a chance to see you functioning in a playful way.
- It allows the students an opportunity to try something bizarre, to experientially step outside their emotional comfort zone.
- Shaking together, led enthusiastically by the instructor, allows the group to experience shared zaniness.
- Fear is not always fear of injury. Fear of failure or fear of looking bad is equally as tough to overcome.

One of the tenets of adventure education is encouraging a consistent effort. Make sure you do not make judgments concerning the quality of a participant's efforts. There is no varsity shaking team.

Find a secluded venue for the chosen day of the "shake." Trying something this emotionally loaded is difficult enough without having peers observing and jeering.

Two-Lip Traverse

Been looking for something zany and off-the-wall for your students to try? Something that requires a huge physical commitment, but no lactic acid build up? A laughter inducing scenario that invites just one more try? I think *Two-Lip* **will serve your humoristic, ice-breaking needs.**

This quirky, photogenic activity requires one simple prop per participant. That prop is fortunately inexpensive and easily transported; a 3 1/2 inch X 1/8 inch rubber band. These rubber bands can be bought by the pound, which means that large group (over 100) participation isn't going to stretch your game budget.

You need to demo this activity first. Remember, it's not how well you do something, it's how well you attempt it. Anticipate your physiognometric gymnastics being greeted by howls of laughter and disbelief.

Using both hands, open your rubber band fully and maneuver it gently over the top of your head, letting it contract slowly so that it comes to rest below your ears and directly on your top lip. **Try this at home in front of a mirror to get the full impact of what you are asking others to attempt.**

Without the use of your hands, or any other prop or appendage, attempt to move the band from your top lip to below your bottom lip. That's it. That's all. Go for it.

A performance tip from someone who's been there...often. Make as much use of your lips and tongue as possible. Other face stretching maneuvers are fun to watch, but accomplish little toward achieving the task. If you have a tongue-stud, cut back on the tongue action.

Distribute the rubber bands and let the fun begin. Some will choose not to participate, so, from a sequencing standpoint, introduce this activity after the group has had the opportunity to "expose" themselves in some other bizarre activity mode, (ex. *The Dog Shake*).

Some facial and oral factors (lip size, facial hair, over bite, tongue dexterity) allow almost instant success. Further challenge these "lucky" players by indicating that moving the band from their lower lip to below their chin and onto the throat is the sine qua non of this soon-to-be Olympic event.

Don't forget to have a couple cameras (still and video) available to record what is basically indescribable.

After finishing up this stretching exercise with adults, indicate that the, by then, well moistened band is theirs to keep as a gift from <u>YOUR COMPANY</u>. Retrieve the bands from all younger students because, well... just do it. Dispose of those rubber bands, and wash your hands before eating.

Balloon Frantic

If you know that one of your adventure teaching/facilitating sessions is going to be observed by an administrator or master teacher, pay close attention to the following game scenario; it's your ticket to an excellent evaluation. Need more guarantee in the excellent direction? This game is highly visual, physical, bizarre, colorful, large group applicable, and encourages communication and coordinated effort. Here's how...

Buy some decent balloons (9-10" balloons go for about ten bucks the gross). There's smaller, less expensive inflatables

to be had, but spring for the extra dollar or two. I know it's probably just me, but I *really* don't like playing this game with small and/or underinflated balloons, it's just not representative of what the game can be. Also, buy balloons of more than one color as the multi-color panoply lends itself to photography and team play.

Pass out the balloons so that each player gets one, (their color choice of course). Blow up a balloon, as a demo, to the size you think will work best for the game, i.e. big, but not too big. **If you blow it up too large the chance of breakage increases proportionally. If you inflate it too little, the bouncing action (time in the air) will be reduced.** Tie off the inflated balloon, perhaps a lesson in itself. You will need about 8-10 extra tied-off balloons. Ask players for help who blow and tie best.

☀ Frantic Rules or Rules for Frantic
(Depending on your centeredness)

- This is a timed event.
- Everyone is on the same team.
- At a signal (Go! still works okay) each player bumps their balloon with an open hand in an upward direction, and continues striking balloons in an effort to keep them off the floor.
- If a balloon hits the floor the instructor yells or blows a whistle. **Yelling is definitely my choice. Whistles are immediately associated with sports and competition. What should you yell? Anything, as long as it's loud.** That yell or whistle is called a BERSERK, and the team is allowed six BERSERKS per FRENZY, (the time it takes to collect those six BERSERKS). Time is stopped after the sixth BERSERK.

- If a balloon hits the floor (receiving a BERSERK, of course) and remains on the floor for over five seconds, that balloon (now referred to as a HECTIC) receives another BERSERK.

- Balloons must be struck, not guided.

- A balloon may not be hit more than three consecutive times by a player.

- Fifteen seconds into the game, and every fifteen seconds thereafter, the instructor introduces an additional balloon into play.

Call STOP! after the sixth BERSERK, announce the time, and indicate that the group has five minutes to prepare for another attempt, (i.e. discuss and make adaptations).

Play your part well. Yell loudly, even hysterically for a BER-SERK. Point with animation at HECTICS. Move about the area and in amongst the "frantic" players. Let them know that you are part of the game, and enjoying the action. *Balloon Frantic* is not a "toss out the balls" game and neither is your role in the game.

I have played *Balloon Frantic* successfully with more than one-hundred people and I'll bet a couple hundred more would function as well. Don't forget to allow enough time for a second attempt.

☀ Variation

The original game of *Frantic*, played with tennis balls on a gym floor, is also a dandy large group game. Play the same rules as above (substitute tennis balls for balloons) except a BERSERK is vocally applied if one of the tennis balls stops

rolling. (All the tennis balls, one per player, are initially started by a facilitator's swift sweeping kick.) The FRENZY (time) ends after the sixth BERSERK.

Use left-over inflatables for other classic balloon games:

- Boop — *The Bottomless Bag Again!?*; page 67
- Gas Attack — (unpublished)
- Passing Gas — *Funn Stuff* #4; page 4
- Balloon Trolley — *QuickSilver*; page 49
- Fire in the Hole — *Silver Bullets*; page 51

Tank

Honestly, the main reason *Tank* is included in this book has to do with its almost 100% success rate with just about any size or kind of group. I have played this game with 10 people and with over 60, with the same result; people really enjoy the action.

You will need one fleece ball per participant and a few extras, just to keep things going when the action gets hot. (If 60+ fleece balls is beyond your budget, ball-up 60+ sheets of paper. Scrap paper balls don't have panache, but the action is practically the same.)

Ask the players to partner-up, i.e. get into pairs. One of the pair becomes the tank, and the other half-a-pair is the driver and weapons expert. The tank gets to hold a fleece ball in each hand and closes their eyes. (Use blindfolds for younger participants.) The driver gets to tell the tank where to go and when to "shoot."

☀ Rules and Such

- The tank should travel in a *bumpers up* position for safety. In this case each "bumper" will be holding a fleece ball.

- All throws are not really throws, rather extensions of the hand that cause more of a put than a throw. This restricted propelling motion is to prevent the tank from winding up and executing an extended throw, with possible rapid hand contact upon another tank.

- If a tank is hit with a propelled fleece ball, the hit tank immediately switches roles with their own driver (tank becomes driver-driver becomes tank) and the game continues.
- There are no time outs, unless you want one.

Caveat — Do not use tennis balls in place of fleece balls; they hurt.

Before the start of the game, allow a few minutes (with no balls in hand) for the pairs to get used to their respective roles and to develop some type of functional transport communication. There is actually very little for you to do once you have explained the rules and started the game. Observe. Take mental notes. Keep it safe. Enjoy.

Jumping Jack Flash a.k.a. Hop Box

There aren't many initiatives that will cause a group of over one-hundred people to develop an immediate sense of team; *Jumping Jack Flash* will do that.

Provide your large group with four "jumping" ropes. **Use retired 25 foot sections of 9mm kernmantle if available, or any kind of rope that has some heft. Wimpy sash cord would not be my first choice, and neither would hefty hawser rope.**

Ask for eight rope turners to situate themselves so that the four held ropes form a rough square, (see illustration). The remainder of the group (30-150+) stand inside the established square waiting for the ropes to begin turning.

Stated objective — As a timed event, see how long it takes for the entire group to exit the square. To exit, each person must make a single jump through *any one* of the four turning ropes.

☀ Associated Rules and Consequences

- Ropes can be turned in either direction, (group choice).

- Each person must make a successful jump through a turning rope. If someone hits the rope causing it to stop, that person, and anyone else making their attempt on that particular jump, must return to the square's interior.

- Simply running through the turning ropes is a big no-no. If someone has made 2-3 honest attempts and is obviously emotionally distraught at the prospect of another miss, allow (encourage) the run-through to take place; usually amidst much applause.

- Each rope turner must also make a jump out of the square. It is the group's responsibility to implement a change of turners for this to take place.

- Multiple simultaneous jumpers is obviously the most efficient way to achieve a lower team time, but if any one of those jumpers cause the rope to stop (a miss), everyone involved in that attempt must return to the square's interior.

Be sure to plan enough participation time to allow a second attempt. The value of a second try, other than capturing one more go at the nostalgic joys of jumping rope, results from recognizing that discussing and applying what you learned the first time will result in a better second effort: more coordinated and choreographed, increased communication, recognized sticking spots, enhanced sense of team, strengths and weaknesses — faster!

Hand Jive a.k.a. Patty Cake

I recently *Hand Jived* with close to one thousand people at a conference center, and if two thousand folks had been there I'm betting it would have been as equally well received.

Ladies, you have been here before. Guys, get set to try something that has not been part of your gender experience base.

This large group happening is based on the parent/infant game *Patty Cake*. As time goes by, and for some sociologic reason, young girls continue to enjoy complex, fast moving, hand related games; boys don't. If you are introducing this

game to a co-ed group you are probably better off not calling it *Patty Cake*. Try *Hand Jive*, much cooler!

Choose a likely person from the group to act as a designated volunteer. Ask that person to stand facing you within arms reach, indicating that you will be initiating a series of arm and hand movements that you would like her to respond to in kind. **Notice I referred to my partner as *her* above. I always choose a female to be my partner for this particular demo, hoping that she has had some experience in jiving hands. On a couple occasions I chose someone who must have been world class at one point in her earlier years; humbling to me, amusing to the group.**

Here's a verbal run through of the hand jive sequence; tedious to read, a lot more fun to try. Remember, you are facing someone and all your movements will be mirrored by your partner.

Stand relaxed with your hands at your side. Slap both of your own shoulders simultaneously, right hand to left shoulder, left hand to right shoulder. Slap your own thighs, right hand to right thigh, left hand to left thigh. Clap both of your own hands together.

What you just tried is a classic jive beginning and is only initiated at the beginning of the hand sequence. Do not repeat this movement unless you make a mistake and want to start over. Notice that you have not yet involved or touched your partner.

After the hand clap (above), extend your right hand (open hand, palm out) toward your partner and clap their also extended right hand. Clap your own hands together, then extend your left hand (open palm as above) to make contact with your partner's extended left hand. This right and left handed movement (that takes much longer to read about than do) is called a cross-clap.

1. Clap your own hands together again once, and this time extend both hands, palms out, to make double palm contact with your partner's extended palms.
2. Clap your own hands together twice and extend both hands, palm out, to make double palm contact (double clap) with your partner's palms.
3. Clap your own hands together three times and make triple palm contact (triple clap) with your partner's palms.

The palm contact with your partner is a distinct clapping movement.

After doing the triple partner clap go back to #2 above and duplicate that movement. After completing #2 go to #1 and complete that movement.

To finish (after completing #1), clap your hands together, do the cross-clap and start over again with #1. The clapping and hand extending continues until you make a mistake or jointly feel like stopping.

It helps to have someone read this text aloud while you and a partner go though the motions.

Back to the large group. Have each person choose an imaginary partner. As you and your volunteer partner go though the hand jive sequence again, ask each person to try and duplicate the movements with their ghost partner. This doppelganger ploy ups the learning curve and cuts down on mistakes, apologies, conversation...

Now go for the real thing. Ask the group to turn left or right and choose a real partner. Go though the sequence one more time slowly with your volunteer partner, asking everyone to also give it a try. Split with your partner, asking her (since she is now an expert) to help you assist the struggling pairs. **Remember it's not how well they follow the hand jive sequence, it's the attempt and how well they associate with one another. Move amongst the pairs offering whatever help seems necessary, also offering lots of enthusiastic feedback as to their high fiving efforts.** Allow about 3-5 minutes for practice, announcing that a hand jive contest is coming up.

The contest. Since everyone has become such classy hand jivers, it would be an aesthetic travesty not to have a chance to display their paired adeptness with a CONTEST! Anticipate hoots, hollers, and Oh noooos! Explain that this contest does not involve speed, rather endurance and concentration. On the GO! signal, each pair initiates the hand jive sequence they know so well. Pairs are allowed to operate as slowly and deliberately as they choose, but one mistake ends their joint attempt, at which point they are out of the contest-honor system, obviously.

Each pair, as they default, become a new entity called a DH, or, Designated Harasser. It is a DH's expanded responsibility to harass the pairs still remaining, attempting to cause them to make a mistake.

☀ Harassing Rules

- No physical contact with the hand jivers allowed.
- Jiver's vision cannot be blocked.
- No screaming or lewd gestures—be nice.

The contest rarely last more than a couple minutes, but with a group of 100+ perhaps a bit longer. Laughter, joshing, and good humor are rampant and expected.

The reason I chose *Hand Jive* as a vehicle for this large game list was its classic nature (some level of adolescent recogni-

tion) and the fact that very few children or adults could claim patty cake skills; leveling the playing field, so to speak.

I particularly like the final twist of encouraging those who "failed" to encourage others to join them in that failure, introducing them to the fun/failure factor, i.e. If you're having fun, failure's not so bad. In an experiential learning situation, allaying fear of failure or looking bad with feel-good fun can be a grand facilitation coup, best enjoyed for what it is, a pedagogic sting.

Tiny Teaching

Because of the post activity sharing, so integral to *Tiny Teaching,* the "large" numbers involved shouldn't exceed 30-40 participants.

Tiny Teaching has become one of my favorite large group/small group activities. Reasons? It segues nicely with another good-fun game called *PDQ* (see page 55), and it's an outstanding one-on-one sharing experience.

Here's all you have to do. Ask the group to break up into pairs. I know it's best to have them pair-up with someone they don't know, but for the sake of fun this time, let 'em pair-up with whomever they please...there's enough valid stuff going on. Teach something, anything, to your paired partner. Use the time allowed to reciprocate a short teaching sequence, i.e. you teach me something, I teach you something.

Like what? Teach what? Anything. Make it interesting, make it fun. Pick something that you do well and teach your new

buddy how to do it. A certain knot. How to make dandelion wine. A dance step. How to put a blade of grass between your thumbs and make a musical (?) sound.

After the 5-7 minute teaching/sharing time, ask the group to reconvene, sit in a circle, then as pairs introduce their partner and share what they learned. This commitment is covered within *challenge by choice*,* so don't expect everyone to want to immediately share with the group, the fact that they shared facts and skills with their partner is significant enough for now.

*Challenge by Choice — Offering a student the opportunity to postpone a personal attempt at a daunting task, be it physical or emotional. The emphasis for all eventual attempts is the attempt itself, not achieving a particular performance level.

Tiny Teaching **with large groups does not lend itself to extensive group sharing; planning on 50+ couples taking the time to share what they just learned is unrealistic and programmatically deadly. Stick with a few of the best pedagogic scenarios, people know when they have been taught something special and will be eager to share it.**

Subway Sardines

This is a limited, large group happening. I doubt that I would go much past 50-60 participants with this activity, and anything near one-hundred could be a mob scene. The title, *Subway Sardines*, **resulted from being reminded what it had been like attempting to squeeze into a subway train during rush hour in Tokyo.**

Standing in the ubiquitous group circle, briefly explain the few moves of this truly simple exercise, then demonstrate one-on-one with a chosen volunteer. Point directly across the circle to the person exactly opposite your position and try to make eye contact, "sunnies" removed, of course. Vocally project that person's first name and have them do the same with your name. If you don't know each other's name, this is a good time to introduce yourself publicly and vociferously.

Walking purposefully and directly across the circle, change places in the arc with your newly named partner. That's it! I told you this was simple.

Suggest that everyone within the circle's arc identify a partner on the opposite side of the circle and introduce themselves from afar. Anticipate lot's of pointing, name shouting, laughter... On a signal from you, all walk across the circle to stand in their reciprocated location. Saying "Howdy" to your partner as you cross would be a friendly thing to do, sharing a few "pardon me's" and "excuse me's" also seems appropriate.

One pair crossing, no problem. Two pair crossing, still no problem. Three pair crossing, better look out. Everyone crossing at the same time—look out for sure! The obvious "white water" results from the inevitable physical contact that's bound to take place with so many people trying to move simultaneously through a restricted area.

Don't encourage the participants to come up with a creative solution that obviates the random contact, let it happen. Do encourage them to handle the bumping bodies in a kind and compassionate way.

During rapidly moving games on the playground, contact is inevitable. In our society there is a very strong emphasis to win or be the best, even in recess pick-up games. To be the best often requires using size, speed and well delivered physical contact. If you are not fast or large, that contact to your body is apt to be delivered in the most efficient and devastating manner possible to gain a competitive advantage. Hip check, trip, push, drag; whatever the action, trust and compassion are not part of a "winning" formula.

Here's an opportunity to practice compassionate contact, to let players know that spontaneous, activity induced contact can be controlled. *Subway Sardines* allows reintroducing fun into activities where compassionate contact is actually a positive part of the game.

If the first crossing was successful, suggest a second crossing where the players speed up their walk a notch. Try that second crossing again, really emphasizing care for each other. If a third crossing is indicated, ask all the players to "walk purposefully" and be, "very aware of all moving bodies."

A final, eyes closed, trip across the circle represents their graduation saunter. Are they ready? Can they handle it? Get a feel from their responses, but you're the ultimate decision maker. Yes? OK! Final trip, eyes closed, walk slowly, and remember, just getting to the other side of the circle is not the goal of this exercise. Go!

"Excuse me." "Pardon me." "I'm so sorry." "My fault."

Yurt Rope

Jim Schoel (a Project Adventure founder) originally came up with the idea of a cooperative hand-in-hand activity called the *Yurt Circle*, essentially a hand-held circle of people supporting one another via the ring-of-tension developed by their connected hands, arms, and bodies. During the early years at PA Jim was much involved in constructing a Yurt* with the students as part of the ongoing adventure curriculum. *Yurt Circle* was a creative, cooperative, symbolic exercise based on that initiative. Many years later, someone had the idea of substituting a rope for hands and arms and the *Yurt Rope* evolved into a popular end of session wrap-up activity.

The first and most important consideration— Choose rope strong enough, rope that will provide the specification strength necessary to handle the applied tension resulting from a large group pulling in-the-round. I have successfully involved 150+ people in the *Yurt Rope* activity, (i.e. the rope didn't break, and the people had a good experience). To insure safely with that many people applying pressure to the rope, I chose 8,000 pound test static kernmantle and doubled it, using a bowline bend as the connecting knot. Allow approximately 30" of rope (people space) per participant when estimating the length needed. Now the fun and function...

Arrange your group in a circle with every one standing to the outside of the circled rope, each person holding the rope with both hands. **This is a "last" activity, so take sufficient time to direct the participant's energy and attention to the team effort that's forthcoming. One or two people fooling around, or doing their own creative thing, can physically and conceptually sabotage what's being attempted.**

With rope in hands, ask everyone to stand comfortably, feet about shoulder width apart. Indicate that on the count of three, everyone should *s l o w l y* begin to lean back against the increasing tension on the rope, attempting to keep their backs as straight as possible, feet solidly in position. **The object is to achieve a substantial individual lean that can only be maintained by everyone cooperatively counterbalancing everyone else. If one person loses control (balance), the group's effort will be forfeit.** Once an acceptable joint lean (acceptable to the participants) is achieved, congratulate the group and tell them they are ready for the next challenge. **Leaning back in a knees-bent, seated position is a sure sign of reduced commitment and trust. Work on it. The activity is unique and visual enough that participants usually don't mind working toward a cooperative goal.**

Ask the circled team to duplicate the lean they just achieved, but this time on the count of three, to try and all sit on the turf (floor) together. Establish the lean, then... one, two, s-l-o-w-l-y SIT. **Results? Some lateral movement, foot slippage, some seated, some collapsed, copious laughter, eagerness to try again. After a couple tries the group usually achieves a 100% simultaneous sit.** Suggest on a similar count they all try to stand at the same time. Considering that gravity helps the sitting process, standing is somewhat more challenging, but it can be done with minimum practice. **Good things are happening, take the time to allow more than one attempt.**

After standing and sitting successfully a couple times, end up with the group all sitting together, legs forward, holding the rope in their laps. Suggest you would like them all to follow your lead and copy your motions. Without gripping the rope (leave it temporarily in your lap), hold your two fists (knuckles up) in front of you (arms partially extended) and laterally rotate both fists clockwise (or otherwise, it doesn't matter), so that the rotation outlines a circle about 12" in diameter. Now, with rope in hand, duplicate with the group what you just mimed. **It's hard to describe what this choreographed rotation of rope looks and feels like, but it produces smiles and comments of Cool! Awesome!**

The creative individualist often provides valuable input toward group decision making, but not for this activity. Performing the rope rotation together demands 100% congruent team work.

Call out "Reverse" and immediately rotate hands and rope in the opposite direction. "Oh, Wow! That *is* cool." Call out numbers to indicate how many rotations should be made before reversing direction. Call out simple arithmetic problems to indicate when the switch should take place. Four minus two - switch after two rotations. Two times two - switch after four rotations, etc.

As a final task, ask everyone once again to follow your lead and attempt to duplicate what you demonstrate. With all participants still sitting, drop the rope and this time do a full body rotational sit up. Starting from a straight-backed sit position, lean forward from the waist as far as you can, then far to the right, then way back (almost lying flat on your back), then far to the left, continuing to the forward lean position. Grab the rope once again, and explain that you are about to start a sitting wave to your right (or left, doesn't matter). The person to your immediate right will begin to duplicate what you initiate as soon as they feel the rope begin to move, etc. around the circle. Make your movements macro, and go slowly so that everyone feels a part of this final and impressive rotational wave.

After the whole group is well into the "wave," reverse direction a couple times and finish in an upright sitting position. If you have a few pithy closing comments for the group, this is an appropriate time to make those observations and/or encourage final reactions from the participants. **Sitting there abundantly smiling, rope in hand, allows a personal connectedness well beyond just the physical hand-to-rope. Take advantage of that moment (schedule for this) and use the time for a brief review of the day.**

*Yurt — A uniquely shaped oval structure made of poles and hides, used as a portable dwelling by nomadic tribes in Asia.

PDQ (Play Determinant Quotient)

I have probably used this playful testing scenario more often than any other activity in my personal bag of tricks. I
remember creating the format and applying the name at a
one-day games presentation in Connecticut, c1977. Since
then I have added to and rearranged the content, establishing a dynamite no-prop activity that serves as well at a
program's onset as it does at the finale. And...it's perfect for
large (100+) groups. (Surprise!)

My patter for this activity involves explaining the rationale
for a pre-experience test, a "test" to scientifically (whatever
that means) determine each participant's proclivity for play.

Before we get going today there is a brief test I would like all of
you to take. Don't fret, the test does not require pencil or paper
and is strictly pass/fail. All you have to do is duplicate what I
demonstrate. Keep your own score. You can include this on
your resume.

How well this activity is received depends almost entirely
upon your enthusiasm, what you ask them to try, and how
proficiently you perform the task. As much as possible include, as tests, something recognizable, some basically useless body manipulation representing a revisitation of childhood or adolescent years.

Explain the format of the testing procedure. You demonstrate
something, then they have the chance to replicate what they
observed. If they can do it (to their satisfaction), PASS. If
they can't, FAIL. Make sure to use these two loaded words
for later discussion reference. Indicate you will start off with
easy tests that progressively become more difficult. Recognize that you have to be able to demonstrate whatever is

chosen as a TEST. Whatever you choose to demonstrate within this format is OK, *as long as you can do it*, and it doesn't offend someone.

First Test: (Finger Snapper)

Ask everyone to snap the center finger of their dominant hand. **Do it yourself first, then watch as all proudly snap their finger several times. Offer hearty congratulations for their attempt and/or performance.**

Second Test: (Alternate Finger Snapper)

Ask everyone to snap the finger of their non-dominant hand. **There's usually a bit of hesitation because many will never have tried to snap a finger of their non-dominant hand, but they will, with a pleased and relieved nonchalance. Point out how easy it is to "look good" by just moving your fingers appropriately but making no sound. Is that cheating? Probably, but acceptable in this context (funn/sharing).**

Third Test: (Finger Popper)

By this time most of the group will be more relaxed and enthusiastically looking forward to the next "test," not caring so much about personal results as anticipating the uniqueness of what they find themselves doing—playing and sharing!

- Hold your extended index finger in front of your face so that you are looking at your finger nail.
- With élan, insert said finger about half way into your mouth.
- Lever the rigid digit forward and out, making a discernible popping sound.

You have upped the experiential ante big-time by expecting this level of oral commitment, but most will enthusiastically pop away, or attempt to do so. Some participants will experience trouble demonstrating a Pop!, producing more of a wet sploochy sound. Without pointing them out (they know who they are) ask the folks who "pop" well to assist their orally challenged teammates by offering suggestions or perhaps demonstrating vis-á-vis the *proper* technique. Allow some time for this important sharing. (Significant caveat—this sharing does not involve inserting someone else's finger in anyone else's mouth. I'm not kidding.)

Fourth Test: (Wiggle Waggle)

Remember, all these tests are things you need to demonstrate. This sequenced scenario does not go over well if you can't joyfully show what you want the participants to attempt. Choose stunts that you can perform toward developing your own PDQ sequence.

Place both hands together in the pray position (palm to palm), approximately a foot in front of your face. Fold down the center finger of each hand, then rotate palms against one another (keeping your extended fingers rigid) until the two folded center fingers oppose one another back-to-back in the classic wiggle-waggle position. **This tricky manipulation is a digital gambit some people remember from their childhood, a parent-taught pastime. You can easily identify these adept folks by their immediate recognition and ability to assume and play with the wiggle-waggle sequence. Use the able players to assist those people who don't have a clue, (obviously those with a childhood experiential hiatus).**

If you are wondering how PDQ can be accepted as a series of tests if everyone is free to offer assistance, let the wonder cease. I assume you have already guessed these bizarre stunts

have nothing to do with a testing sequence, rather representing an invitation to play, to share, to cooperate. But don't tell, we're not done yet, and to be honest, the participants don't seem to care. Check out the level of participation and enjoyment. Good things are happening. Keep testing.

Fifth Test: (Head Wrapper)

OK, how's everyone doing? Are you happy with your score to this point? Try to up your success ratio with this doozy of a challenge. Extend your arms to the front with palms about 6" apart. Turn your hands over so that the backs of your hands are juxtaposed. Cross your extended arms so that now your palms face one another and grasp both hands together, fingers intertwined. Move both hands together, first down then up toward your face, putting you in the identical preliminary position so common to a trust fall. So positioned, the task is to try and insert your entire head through the area between your crossed forearms without letting your fingers disengage. **Can't see the cranial insertion area? It's right between where your wrists cross. Think it can't be done? Drop by the *High 5 Adventure Learning Center* office and I'll give you a quick demo. I told you the tests were getting harder. In a group of fifty you may have 2-3 who can complete this contortionist maneuver. Be alert to conscientious attempts and apply copious praise for the efforts being expended. Considering the high level of shared failure, the concept of laughter *with*, rather than laughter *at*, becomes more meaningful.**

Sixth Test: (Where's the Sausage?)

Since everything presented up to this juncture has consisted of a visual pass/fail, it's time for a conceptual test, the result of which will only be manifest to the test taker. Simply hold extended index fingers (two) in front of your face (about 16" from your eyes), so that finger tips barely touch. Look directly at the contact point between your two fingers and if you see a small link sausage (about an inch long) visually inserted between the tips of your fingers, you have passed the test. **Anticipate comments of, "I SEE it!" to "Whaaaat?" and facial looks either wreathed in smiles or wrinkled in consternation. To help those still searching for the sausage, suggest they look directly past their fingers to a point on the floor or wall. "Oh yeah, I see it now. How cool!" Sadly, some will never see the sausage, and if that includes you, I apologize for the frustration and suggest that you drop this test from your repertoire.** To stimulate further fun, for those AT ONE with the sausage, suggest a slight separation of finger tips in order to see the sausage *float in mid air*. **More ecstatic comments of "Wow, I didn't know I could do that, etc." As a fantastic and completely extraneous finale to this digital folderol, ask if anyone can:**

1. Visually identify the sausage, then...
2. Touch that tube of mini-meat with their tongue without visually losing contact.

Have a camera available, because this is a facial happening not be believed

Seventh Test: (Hand Hooter)

Remember blowing into your cupped hands as a kid producing a hooting sound? No? Then you aren't going to like this final test. With your hands cupped together, blow across (not into) the opening that occurs between your juxtaposed thumbs, producing a characteristic loon-like sound that is both the boon of children and the bane of parents. **This is pass/fail folks, it either happens or it doesn't, and by this time your participants should be fully imbued in the concept of failing forward and be eager to learn the intricacies of cupped-hand**

music. You will probably have at least 6-8 people in a group of 50-60 who can produce a verifiable hand-hooting sound. Use those willing virtuosos to spread their expertise in a ripple effect of extemporaneous sharing.

Finish this particular segment of time by explaining to the group that PDQ was obviously not a test, rather an invitation to play, an invitation to share.

I've chosen **PDQ** as the final activity write up because it has represented such a useful part of my personal bag of tricks over the years. The various "tests" have literally saved my professional bacon countless times when I initially needed something experiential to capture a large audience's imagination and enthusiasm. As a strong finisher, **PDQ** has also consistently proven its curriculum worth by allowing large and small groups to end a program day with knowing smiles and wanting more.

Have you ever heard the expression... How much is a new idea worth? Ultimate worth has to do with how you use the idea, but I hope the ideas and suggestions in this small book add up to more than just dollar value for you.

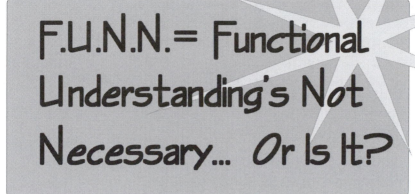

F.U.N.N.= Functional Understanding's Not Necessary... Or Is It?

Gloree Rohnke

This small book is filled with adventure-based activities for large groups, 30 to 100 plus participants. The variety of games and problem-solving activities present an assortment for effective sequencing. The flow of activities allows you to move from the basic aim of a program plan to more complex topics. The fundamental adventure sequence recommends you begin your group's experience with comfort building icebreakers, followed by safety developing "relaxers," communication builders, trust shapers, and problem-solving initiatives, finally wrapping-up with closing activities.

Effective sequencing of adventure activities encourages participants to interact positively, work for a common goal, act creatively, and accept the personal challenge to take increased levels of risk while engaged in a fun and non-competitive activity. However, as you plan your session and select your activities, another decision remains: Will this be a recreational or F.U.N.N, play day or is the client's goal to blend fun and awareness for personal development?

The answer to this question initiates another possibility. Do the facilitators need to guide a reflective process and complete the four-phased Experiential Learning Cycle? The cycle is a learning process originated at Massachusetts Institute of Technology by David Kolb in 1984. The basic theory explains that learning occurs with 1) a natural or contrived *experience*, which generates 2) a critical *inspection* of the experience from which the participant 3) gains useful *insights that connect* with previous life events leading to 4) a*mending* behavior and/or understanding that is then *integrated* into his or her life practice.

Since the objectives of the program influence your plan, you are faced with either general sequencing or whether activities need to be selected to build upon one another developing an Experiential Learning Spiral of learning events that promote greater personal awareness. (G. Rohnke, 2000) The impact of adventure philosophy in a learning community can be remarkable considering the changes that develop within the group's dynamics. However, for a large number of participants in a short term session of only a few hours, awareness building is usually the most you can plan for and any other outcomes are "icing" on your programmatic cake.

Over the years, it has been a privilege to observe Karl and study his style in various venues. Generally, in a large group program he uses a facilitator led discussion to "debrief" his groups. This allows the participants to look at the facts and features of the experience. You will notice throughout this book that Karl is resourceful as he moves through his program, taking advantage of contrived or natural "teachable moments" that frequently occur through his presentation. Karl has an intuitive and well-honed ability to integrate purpose, fun, and learning as he teases the participants' beliefs through an artful combination of thought provoking questions, relevant vignettes, and well-placed insights that motivate new understanding.

Sometimes, however, it is programmatically beneficial for the participants to be in smaller, informal task groups, with or without assigned leaders. Smaller groups encourage 'safe spots' amidst a real or perceived human throng where participants have the opportunity to reflect on the activity and exchange observations, perceptions, and insights with one another. This interaction is reflective processing that demonstrates a critical thinking process which broadens and deepens understanding, enhancing the individual and, ultimately, the group's learning experience.

Reflection is a thinking process that people naturally conduct when they learn through cause and effect. As experiential educators, our role is to guide the process so that individuals can expand their learning by sharing and listening to others completing the same, often concurrent, cycle of thinking. By presenting reflective experiences, participants are offered opportunities to *discover for themselves* a greater depth of learning and to build upon the lessons of the program sessions, creating a spiral of experiential learning.

The following suggestions create reflective processing episodes to stimulate and deepen personal awareness regardless of group size. In addition, some facilitators and programs are limited by operating within the context of a large group discussion, making it helpful to have some alternative suggestions for meeting the program's goals. Please use the examples, make your own evaluation, then design the use of the reflection tasks where they fit into your program.

Each of the following activities present guidelines and many are linked to at least one of the activities from Karl's chosen anthology. Most recommend that the groups be subdivided into more manageable numbers for group sharing. Several activities playfully initiate individual contemplation or evaluation. Some tasks will ask the participants to complete the experiential process to accomplish the activity and to apply the change of perspective just gained.

Following the themes of Karl's activities, relevant questions are offered for the following task examples These are divergent or open-ended questions that will prompt varied responses rather than produce the standard "right" answer. With short programs and large groups, you are often challenged for the time needed to develop in-depth processing. Many times you are only able to provide events that inspire observations without the guidance of how to connect or apply that lesson. Trust the process, motivated participants will naturally complete the learning for themselves at some level.

Body Indicators

Need a technique to get a quick response to those simple facilitator review questions? Try out these quick indicators.

※ Thumbulator

Ask the group to form a circle or arrange themselves in a manner where all members can see one another. Tell them that their thumb is to become a 'Thumbulator,' a measuring tool to demonstrate the level of satisfaction the participant achieved from the previous activity or to indicate their response to any number of simple questions the facilitator might ask. To use their Thumbulator, either the left or right close-fisted hand is held in front of the participant with the thumb extended at the desired level. They will indicate their response on the count of "One-two-three, Show!" The Thumbulator scale is based on "Thumbs Up" to indicate the member was a hundred percent satisfied. A

"Thumbs Down", consequently, indicates that the participant was unsatisfied and anywhere in-between would indicate the various levels of satisfied to unsatisfied the individual member is in response to the question.

Example

As an intervention, halt the group during a game of *Pairs Tag*, introduce the Thumbulator, and ask:

- How do you feel about the boundaries of the game?
- How safe did you feel playing the game?
- Would you like to resume the game with broader boundaries?

At this point, you could expand the boundaries, perhaps remind folks about "walking" safely while playing and then resume the game. Of course, at the end of the game you could ask them to demonstrate how much fun they had playing.

☀ Handbulator

This approach would work similarly to the *Thumbulator*, however, this time the group would be holding hands as each member responded within the group. Hands above their heads would represent the highest level of fun and hands down to the ground would be the lowest. Anything in-between could indicate any manner of responses!

Example

After completing *Two-Lip Traverse,* you could ask the group:

- What was the level of F.U.N.N. you experienced during the activity?

Variation

You could also add sound effects to this technique to coordinate with the hand movements: hands up with happy sounds, and hands down with grumbles, etc.

☀ Puppet Personality

In this quick indicator, the individual communicates his or her response to an activity or a series of activities using their entire body to respond, The responses are open to interpretation, stimulate thinking, and offer the opportunity for some playful antics.

Example

After completing the following sequence of warm up activities—*Share a Stretch, Heel Clicker, and Gotcha!*—ask you group to demonstrate:

- First, how he or she felt when she arrived
- Second, how he or she is feeling at the present.

This can then be an opportunity to offer a quick comment on the value of play or check-in to see if they are ready to move on to another activity!

Discussion Alternatives

Throughout the book, Karl uses intervals to offer or invite comments and as we have seen, at the end of many activities there is the opportunity for facilitator led discussions. Depending on goals and time available, these conversations can range from reactions to the activity or be guided to complete a full learning cycle.

Example #1

A suggested reflection sequence for *Balloon Frantic* using only main topic questions:

- What was your favorite part of the game?
- Was there any part of the game that you found uncomfortable?
- How well did the group operate as a team?
- What could this group do to work together as a team to improve their time for the next attempt?

Example #2

After completing the activity *Tank, say:*

- Explain which role you preferred, tank or driver.
- Was it OK for anyone who used Challenge by Choice® and took a peek during the activity?
- What can we do to help people feel safe? Why do we trust some people more than others?
- How can we use an activity like *Tank* to value other people's sense of trust?

✳ *Thought Spots*

This small group task allows your participants to briefly exchange their thoughts about the activity, lessons, or session.

Between activities, ask the participants to move about randomly. Call a halt. Tell them to place themselves in pairs or triads with the people near them. Indicate that this a 'Thought Spot' and ask them to share their thoughts as they respond to a previous activity or experience. Keep the conversations at about two or three minutes to allow each to speak briefly, then move on.

Variation

Follow the above directions, except ask the participants to respond to a guiding question:

Examples

- *Everybody's It*: What was the best/worst part of the game for you?

- *Weird Walking/Categories:* How were these two activities similar?

- *Dog Shake*: How is this activity connected to school, learning, or working in teams?

- *Subway Sardines:* How does this activity mirror events or experiences in your real life?

- *PDQ:* How do you define success?

Variation

This task could also be used as a quick pause within an activity, especially if there are issues developing. Ask what the group sees happening and discuss a possible solution. This allows a group to monitor its own progress.

※ Metaphor Mombo

This time, after the group meanders around the room backwards, using their favorite animal walk or some other alternative motion, call a stop, and direct them to form into random duos or triads. Ask participants to create, then share out a single metaphor that expresses a key learning from the previous activity.

Examples

Up Chuck, Pairs Tag, Jumping Jack Flash, or Projected Proverbs.

✳ Primary Perception

In this instance, ask your group to form into random groups of three. Each member will answer a guiding question from a specific perspective. One member will respond from the "Looks Like" perception. The other two will each take either the "Sounds Like" or "Feels Like" perspective. Allow about five minutes at most, then move on to the next activity. Use questions that challenge the participant to evaluate the activity, define their perceptions, and draw an insight from the experience.

Examples

- *Dog Shake*: What were you thinking while watching the facilitator demonstrate this activity?
- *Galloping Hands*: What were the benefits (or challenges) of competition during the Team A and Team B contest?
- *Weird Walking*: How did your feelings change about crossing the open area?
- *Hog Call:* What were you thinking halfway across the field?

✳ Reverse Reflection

This task offers the participant a chance to look at circumstances from another perspective. Ask the group members to find a partner. Using a facilitator posed question, have each pair member choose a role and then respond from another person's perspective. For example: Teachers could become parents or administrators, men could see through the eyes of women (and vice versa) or adults could respond as a teen, or a teen as a parent.

Examples

- *Jumping Jack Flash:* Do you think people should be encouraged to try or left to their own decision about participating?
- *Yurt Rope:* How important is cooperation in a classroom (or in the workplace)?
- *Galloping Hands*: Who is the most important player on the team?
- *Projected Proverbs:* What does a group (class, unit, sports team) need to work together?

☀ Share Swappers Dance

This is really a string of activities that encourages your participants to have fun as they literally have to "think on their feet." Introduce this dance series by demonstrating each step and then asking the participants to rehearse them. Once mastered, ask participants to think of a word or short phrase to explain or describe a key insight he or she gained during the previous activity. Begin the Share Swappers dance step and then, if desired, call out another dance step, alternate among the steps, and finishing with the *Partner Promenade*.

Variation

Each of the dance steps could be used alone if desired.

Swappers Left

Line your group up into a large circle. Divide the line in Pairs (be sure to find a partner for any single participant) and have them face one another. Ask the pairs to reach out with their left hands as if to shake hands. Instead, tell them they will use the square dance step that has participants:

- Clasping left to left hands as they walk past their temporary partner.
- Then, extend their right hand to clasp the right hand of the next person in line.
- The participants will then repeat this process as they move from person to person (developing a new pair briefly) around the circle always alternating the hand they extend to each person.

Once they have the dance step mastered, indicate that each time a pair extends both their left hands toward each other, each member of the pair will swap one word or a two or three short word phrase regarding a key *insight* they gained from the activity. Be sure to demonstrate so that they can see what is expected. Once participants have completed several contacts to share, call out *Partner Promenade*.

Do What Did

During this dance step, the pairs fold their arms across their chests and circle around each other moving alternately from face to face, side to side, back to back, side to side and face to face before moving on to the next person. During their *Do What Did,* the members exchange a single word or short phrase describing an *emotion* they felt during the activity.

Partner Promenade

The position required to "dance" around the circle this time is accomplished by a pair of participants (either of the moment or pre selected for a special connection) who move into a side by side, face forward position in which left hands of the pair will be clasped in front of the left partner and the right hands will be clasped to the side *and over the shoulder* of the left partner. Traveling in this dance position around the circle, the pair can conduct a short conversation, exchanging how they could *apply* their individual key insight into a new situation.

Example Activity Choices

Pairs Tag, Quick Touch, Tank, Hand Jive, Tiny Teach, Subway Sardines, Projected Proverbs, Balloon Frantic, Weird Walking, Up Chuck, Dog Shake, Yurt Rope...

☀ Choose Your Corner

This activity will need flip-chart paper or newsprint, markers, and tape. If using an outside venue, select volunteers to be "poster pals" or find four well placed trees! Set up four poster "corners" in your play area with up to four sets of pre-selected statements (single words), listed singly on a large sheet of flip-chart paper that has been folded back upon itself lightly to cover the words until they are posted.

Explain to the group that each of us typically identifies with a role, preference, or certain position on a particular topic or issue. In up to four rounds, ask participants to respond to a question or take a stand on an issue related to the activity. This is done by posting statements that represent four different viewpoints on the same topic. The participants will select the posted viewpoint with which they are most closely aligned and move to the chosen corner in response to the facilitator's prompt.

Keep this simple and quick for a play day. However, if there is enough time, ask the participants to discuss with the others in their "chosen corner" why they made their choice, Then, move on to the next prompt.

Example

Weird Walking/Categories

- Weird Walking and Categories was like:
    - Bike riding
    - A new school (job)
    - Clothes shopping
    - Bungee jumping

- I found both activities:
    - Similar
    - Different
    - Confusing
    - Enlightening

- When I make choices, I am like:
    - The Red Baron
    - Mickey Mouse
    - Goofy
    - Wonder Woman

- In a group, I am a:
    - Cruise Ship
    - Canoe
    - Motor Boat
    - Kayak

Variation

As a closing activity the groups could ask a question of those in another corner.

Thought Spiralers

The following reflection tasks encourage the participants to complete the critical thinking phases of the Experiential Learning Cycle. A sequence of well chosen activities can promote their thoughts into a spiral of learning and/or awareness.

☀ Artistic License

This is an old stand-by with a new name that spurs the participant through their thought process to accomplish the activity. Split your group into smaller, more manageable mini-groups. Provide art materials and ask the group to create collectively, a T-shirt motto, a record label, a book title, a banner, a flag, a newspaper headline, or a magazine advertising slogan that would:

- Reflect how the group experienced the activity.
- Indicate how the group members would use their insight from the experience to change the future.

Designate a spokesperson from each group to display and explain their creative work.

Example Activities

Quick Touch, Projected Proverbs, Tank, Tiny Teach, Balloon Frantic, Hand Jive, Up Chuck, Jumping Jack Flash, Galloping Hands

Variation

This could be done individually, however, it would require substantial time to explain to the larger group unless it was accomplished in smaller sub groups.

✳ Review, Link, and Use

Divide the large group into sub groups. Ask them to review the current activity, link it to another lesson from the day, and create a one minute skit demonstrating how to use the lesson to improve a future situation.

✳ Celebration Time

Ask the participants to select a partner. Instruct them to create a movement and sound of celebration, something simple that could be used throughout the day. Explain that periodically, the facilitators would exclaim, "Celebration Time." At that point, the participant's locate their partners, do their movements, and take a minute each to share a personal moment of celebration observed during the workshop.

Variation

This is a nice activity for a final closure of the workshop experience (and a perfect segue to the next section).

Closures

✳ Mementos

Provide a symbolic object or materials to create an item the participants can then take with them upon departure that will be a reminder, bolstering the experience or lessons gleaned from the day. Marbles, paper chain sections, beaded pins, painted rocks, yarn bracelets, certificates, photographs, post cards, and poetic or musical lyrics are some examples of items that could be used.

✳ Story Glove

At the end of the workshop, provide four inch or larger colored hands for each participant and pencils or markers. Ask them to add a thought to one finger for each significant activity from their day, then sign the hand, Ask the participants to "line-up in a circle" and pat their neighbor on the back for a job well done.

Variation

Pass out the colored hands early on the day of a short program. Participants are then asked to add a thought or comment on each finger as they complete an activity. At the end of the session, ask them to randomly share a few thoughts from their hands as you remind them of an activity. Finally, ask them to pat themselves on the back for a job well done.

☀ Double Bubble

Review the activities of the day with the participants. Provide a small bottle of bubbles and a wand for each person. Allow time for participants to blow bubbles into the air around them. Then ask them to pick one highlight, significant lesson, or perception gained from the workshop experience, and, looking at the bubbles, to define the shape, color and texture of the experience as it relates to their life.

Variation

This is an opportunity for participants to make a pledge for future change, blow bubbles, and commit it to the universe. The bottle of bubbles can be taken home as a memento of their experience or commitment.